GW00496567

daybreak

cusp tanka 2022

daybreak

cusp tanka 2022

Joy McCall

A Stark Mountain Press Book

daybreak
cusp tanka 2022

joy@joymccall.plus.com

Cover photo © Kate Franks, Calgary,
Canada 2023

Cover design by Larry Kimmel

ISBN: 979-8-3901928-5-6
Imprint: Independently published

Don't turn away.
Keep your gaze on the bandaged place.
That's where the light enters you.

If light is in your heart
You will find your way home.

I am a fish. You are the moon.
You cannot touch me, but your light
can fill the ocean where I live.

Rumi

wind and a clear sky
quite cold on my morning walk
a sliver of moon
one purple crocus open
it's enough … and not enough

for Joy

Tom Sexton, Anchorage, Alaska

Foreword

I find a special quality in your tanka, a beautiful quality. Even though I feel most nature tanka are sentimental, yours are sharp and concrete; and your co-causal awareness is one that few people know about – pain/joy, light/dark, happiness/sadness–yes that is always with us. But with knowing you, all is Joy.

> where is it?
> tell me, wise Joy,
> where truth is –
> buried in ghosts?
> hidden in dark corners?

> a dark sky above me
> and a yellow moon
> I know
> you would have loved it
> with black crows overhead

Sanford Goldstein Japan

Gifts from poet friends –

<>

Dawn wounds the darkness
light bleeds from the east
bringing with it hope

on the darkest of nights
a full moon
rises above
the trees

lighting a candle
joyful memories
challenge the grief

and just like that
the darkness fled
from the light

after the darkness
has faded away
we can bathe
in the light
that renews our souls

Steve Wilkinson, Yorkshire – poet and
editor of The Bamboo Hut and Take 5ive

in my dream
I am there
at the beginning of the world
& the swans
turn into stars

& the stars
turn into swans

Tony Marcoff, Surrey, England

grandma's here!
shouts the excited child
at the window
the sun peeks through –
it's a brand new day

Michael Lester, Los Angeles

first light
and again I'm brewing coffee –
like an ant
on a moebius strip
this dailiness

Larry Kimmel, Massachusetts

wondering
where to buy
a magic carpet
I warp the loom with words
and weave my own

Jenny Ward Angyal, North Carolina

we are defined
by the light – drawing our edges
we begin and end
at a great dark doorway
backlit from another world

Kate Franks, Alberta, Joy's daughter

high above the holy roof
a pale moon shining
we travel
by the light of the moon
the road becomes clear

when the day breaks
we stop at the old inn
there we rest
the sound of bird-song
lifts our souls

Joy and Andy McCall, Norwich

bird on a power line
cloudy sky above
watching   watching
waiting   waiting
bird on a power line

Jonathan Day, Alpine, Oregon

shocked by
tangerine green
sunrise
awake from doldrums
siren of spring

Carole Johnston, Lexington, Kentucky

the night train
blows through town,
scattering leaves
and my dreaming, too,
down the iron rails

Michael McClintock, Clovis, California

my deer family
wandering
the cold tract of night
this daily search
for light

Tom Clausen, Ithaca, New York

daybreak
cusp tanka 2022

January – June

loud music
and New Year fireworks
I am not sorry
to leave the sad last year
far behind me

her brown hair
turning white
her breath
freezing the strands
in the cold Calgary park

(Kate)

broken
I look for healing
kintsugi –
but where is the gold
to fill all the cracks?

do all things in life
come at a cost?
do we have to choose
whether to pay the price
or close the door?

reliving
games I played
as a child
'I sent a letter
to my love'

I thought
happiness
was the goal
now I see
it is to be good

there are things
we know
but can't believe
that one day
even the sun will die

the mountain
ahead of me
is too high to climb
I sit in the foothills
counting blessings and tears

Meat Loaf dead
Steinman gone
still, so many roads
lead me back
to Amherst

giving birth
in that college town
all I hear is
'I won't look back
at the altar shine'

(Meat Loaf song)

I dream of water snakes
caught and drying out
on the bank –
I gather them and dive
back into the river

my eyes
filling with tears
catch the flight
of a dark butterfly
among the bare trees

when I crashed
the abbey fell
into the sea
still, the tower stood
and my prayers rose

sad, I draw
zen cards at midnight –
sorrow, healing
completion
letting go

I close my eyes
and a daydream comes
I'm halfway up a hill
going to a ruined shrine
the sun is on my face

wild storms
dark clouds
the sky
as troubled
as my heart

the horse and the doe
hide in the shadows
the bright eyes
of the black raven
watch over them

(Wendy, Joy, Kate)

sitting by the holy fire
with Meat Loaf songs
cranked up loud
echoing around the rafters ...
'heaven can wait'

sometimes
I take down a book
from years past
and read – and find myself
hiding in the pages

no train
rumbling in the night
just the wind
howling down
the railway tracks

my father
when overwhelmed
by work, sighed
'I have to go see
a man about a horse'

he has a dream
of living in the wilds
of America
travelling the trains
like Boxcar Willie

the foot
I am missing
is twitching
it's time to sleep
and dream a wild dance

past midnight
I should sleep
oh but ...
the wind, the owls
the little train

midnight
old motorbikes
a loud owl
I'm caught between
town and country

one nephew
covered in Escher ink
another
fiery dragons ...
I settle for kanji

the old man
in far away Japan
bearded, bemused
sometimes forgets me
and our tanka

(for Sandy)

I would
want a heart,
not of gold
but of rain, wind
and feathers

the wild beauty
of the blackness
of the bare trees
against the light
of the morning sky

looking out
from his cliff-top cave
to the lowerlands
the old hobgoblin
starts to cry

the full snow moon
shines on the old asylum
and in its light
the lunatics still sing
dancing down the long hall

(Thorpe St. Andrew abandoned asylum)

the locum doctor
says my neck pain
comes from grief
and blame and it is time
to let it go

silent
a shadow bird flew
across my room
leaving no song
and no feather

two decades
since last my foot
touched the earth
yet I feel the soil,
the stones, the bones

I long
for a hermitage
in far mountains
with the cry of the deer
and the wind in the pines

there is an ocean
of grief deep down
and small gladness
floating, drifting
on the surface tides

stormy February
the wind howling
through the trees
a small dark butterfly
lands on my window

so many
kinds of dancing –
I love best
the honey bees
on the meadowsweet

these days
I forget things
that matter ...
a tiny gnat
lands on my hand

there's a great house
made of sand in the field
the storm comes
the wind rises –
the house blows away

how do I do
what she asked of me
and carry her graciousness
and not her suffering
written on my soul?

(for Wendy)

the story of a pilgrim
pulling his life's threads
together
tying the knot
settling his soul

(Gerry)

the sailor
marooned on dry land
yearns for the sea
for the wind in the sails
for the wide open spaces

(M. Kei)

hemp balm
eases the pain
and brings sleep
but oh the puzzles
of tangled dreams

she climbed on her bike
to look over the fence
at the wild ponies
and she smiled and said
'theirs is my journey too'

(Wendy)

on hold
to the hospital line
then a quiet nurse
answers and sings
'Happy Birthday to you'

on the seesaw
summer and winter
joy and pain
night and day
you and me

white cloud horse
galloping
racing across
the dark sky
not a fence in sight

why I would love
to be Ryōkan :
nature
solitude
silence

my joints
clicking and crunching
like the pebbles
washed by tides
of salt water

all winter long
the brown moth
flits by my window ...
of course you know
what I'm thinking

(In many Native American cultures, they
considered moths to be messengers from
the spirit world, especially from those that
have passed on).

mass graves
in Mariupol
are we back
to the dark ages
or have we never left?

if only soldiers
and the young gang men
would beat their knives
like the swords of old
into plough-shares

(And he shall judge among the nations, and
shall rebuke many people: and they shall
beat their swords into plowshares, and their
spears into pruning hooks: nation shall not
lift up sword against nation, neither shall
they learn war any more. Isaiah 2:4)

the full Worm Moon
lighting up my room
gets its name
from those small things
crawling up from the ground

sometimes nature
sends a silent message
when I most need one –
no matter how hard the road
there is beauty, there is hope

a coach load
of scared orphans
from the war zone
land in Scotland and meet
open arms, kindness and hope

she brings
smiles and hope
laughter
and understanding
and sunshine

(Kate)

pain and struggle
wars and rumours of wars
but outside my window
the first dancing rattling bag
white against the violets

we plant
rosemary cuttings
in the churchyard –
remembrance
is sad and glad

in the old church
pale light through stained glass
quiet still air
we light candles
for our loved ones

black bird
picking insects
from white birch bark
just like life –
light and dark

the last day
of her holiday
tired and sad
we play our worst
Scrabble game ever

on her farewell card
a garden girl, a rabbit
a snail, birds. worms
butterflies and bees ...
rain clouds, green leaves

(Kate)

in all the world
and across the land
and in my heart
love and grief
go hand in hand

a mother
and three laughing children
wave and shout
'zdravstvuyte'
as they pass my window

('hello' — many families in Norwich
have opened their hearts and homes
to Ukrainian refugees)

reading
his river poems
I gaze at rain clouds
and long for silence
far from this noisy city

(Tony Marcoff)

as I fall asleep
the face of an old man
smiles at me
with missing teeth –
who is he?

a small branch
fell from the witch-hazel tree
and called to me
to take it to the meadow,
divining

the more I learn
the more I ache
for this good earth ...
ignorance
is a kind of bliss

growing beside
this busy road
slow-ripening sloes
and a crooked tree
bearing figs

four rough
and dirty lads
smelling of weed
pass me by, stop
and ask – 'are you OK?'

outside
Heaven's gate
the rivers of grief
flow over the hills
back down to earth

the moon woke me
and I watched it
through the branches
of the silver birch
and heard her voice –

//

I see the moon
the moon sees me
God bless the moon
and God bless me

(Wendy about 4 years old)

(Joseph Ritson the author of the rhyme
died in Hoxton asylum built in1695; at
the age of 51.)

the moonlight
the daylight
the white clouds –
she said: *'I am light,
watch me shine'*

(Wendy)

I love daylight
and the blackbird's song
but a bit later please
I'm not yet finished
with my night's sleep

I am
lopsided
off-balance,
mind and body
'on the huh'

(Norfolk saying)

the man with Downs
on the river green
says he is scared
of falling in the water :
'my name is Bridge'

//

he asks my name
I say Joy
and he laughs
'I guess you are
afraid of sorrow then?'

the ancient
clay marbles
in the birdbath
the magpie stole them
one by one

we take the small cross
from the churchyard
to our oregano patch
and an English robin
perches there, singing

my tattoos –
things that break the rules :
flying fish
diving birds
swimming snakes

as my gaunt teacher
wrote, threatening
with the ruler
'Joy must try harder
and stop day-dreaming'

things die
and somehow live again
the trees, the weeds
the bees, the butterflies ...
us?

the great Ganges
rushes down hills
and across plains
and tumbles the rocks –
shiva lingam

I thought
I was a mad March hare
until the Cree shaman said
you are doe ... and like so many,
you may be road kill

I grow older
on the surface
and yet
within me, a child sings
a girl dances

dandelion seed heads
drifting on the breeze
please carry
these sorrows
away with you

the young vicar
laid his hand
on my shoulder
but no words came –
is silence a prayer?

I hear his voice
upstairs, talking
to the cat –
'leave that spider alone
I need sleep'

(Andy)

I breathe deeply
the lovely scent
of goose grass ...
and spend the night
coughing

high on the tower
of the old church
on the Norfolk coast
a mother and daughter
watch the waves

I wake at
02:22
and find myself
in 2022
lost in numbers again

Mum's hand sewn bag
Wendy's turquoise bowl
Kate's woodcarving
Andy's vintage hare, a painting, stones ...
some things matter a lot

gnats rising up
from the hedges
in clouds
but where are the swifts
to come swooping by?

sadness
my body's pain
moonrise
the blackbird's song
the little train

a thunderstorm
and the first rain
in weeks
I hear the thirsty ground
singing praise to the clouds

brick weave
clean and tidy
or filled with weeds
and busy picking birds?
I know which I choose!

strange light
through the dark trees
and the cripple limped
down the long hill
laughing to himself

a little girl
down railway lane
showing me a stone
she found on the marsh
says 'it is very old'

the wild patch
that men ploughed down
grows wild again
and hums with bees
on meadowsweet and mustard

mum said
'sometimes
the only way
through trouble
is jiggery-pokery'

//

and dad said
'you're up late
it's ten o'clock
get yourself to bed
lickety-split'

the clock creeps
slowly to midnight
the witching hour
I sing softly to myself
'now the green blade rises'

as I shuffle,
the fool slips
out of the tarot deck –
where is wisdom
these unsettled days?

Sunday sounds :
collared doves cooing
blackbirds singing
ambulance sirens
matins bell ringing

not knowing
what else to do
I say a prayer
light a candle
and send dark chocolate

the cards say
if I go with the flow
with courage
there are possibilities
I have not even imagined

yellow hawkweed
and an old Triumph
and starlings
in the June sunshine
somehow they all go together

I dreamed again
the winged seal
rising up
to the sea surface
and taking to the sky

I look at the old scroll
on my wall – the crane
at island's end
and I wonder, is there a bird
waiting to take my soul to heaven?

he says
I am lovely
I say I am
scraggy and old
maybe we are both right

I still see mum
sharing chocolate pudding
pointing to heaven
wearing the silver bracelet I made
'love, hope, charity'

(she died an hour later)

reading Lu Yu
I long to share his white tea
with rose petals
raspberries, mallow flowers
and spring water

//

or to climb
all those steps
to 'heaven's gate'
and drink
from the clear spring

(Tianmen Mountain, China)

I missed
the old hawkweed
uprooted in the storm
but now where it grew,
a new bright yellow hope

when things are empty
and we refill them
that's restoring –
water bowls, bread bins
hearts and souls

new streetlights
solar powered
gentler light
sleep comes more easily
and I can see the stars

these times are often
difficult and sad
and yet ...
all over the patio, weeds
dancing in the sunshine

I count
seven yellow flowers
on the hawkweed
no wonder it seems
holy to me

the ruined shrine
home to mosses
and wild deer
still calls my name
begging me to come

this the age
not of aquarius
but of reiwa
not of rebellion
but peaceful harmony

(Reiwa – official Japanese name for this era –
peaceful harmony)

I wake at night
my fingers stuck
and unbending
like my grief,
my stilled body

I am a mouse
scurrying into the hollow log
where I sleep
and wait for dusk
and the dark safety

the black bird sat
singing at my window all day
I guess he knew
today was two decades
of stilling loss

we change
the ancient name
of our Old Yard
now we live
in Hawkweed House

'the cradle
for the body is nature'
said Susumo ...
I settle to sleep in
hawkweed and feathers

solstice morning
I think of circles
water bowls
mandalas, henges ...
hawkweed

once I sat
by Long Meg
and her daughters
my hand resting
on the cup-and-ring

the spirit of jizo Niko
in the fire and flame
sparked
and children danced
and dark swallows flew

Sunday dusk
the evensong bell rings
the smallest falcon
flaps her wings
and takes flight

he reads aloud
old nursery rhymes
and the child within
comes out laughing
reciting with him

(for Jonathan)

we sat in the garden
in the evening peace
and wild swifts
came screaming
low over our heads

St,John's Wort, hemp
cloves and tumeric
frankincense and ginger
sandalwood, lavender
rosemary ... solace!

until the breath
leaves our lungs
and the beat
leaves our hearts ...
let us love and laugh

the turning of the year …

July – December

where two friends danced
in the High Ash fields
metal detectors find
hoards of gold Roman coins –
we should have dug, not danced

three young deer
grazing too close
to the road
he walks gently near
and they move to safety

crooked and bent now
the prickly berberis
dark berries for the birds
bright blossom for the bees
small spiky green leaves

my friend
the Catholic monk
bedbound and ill
spends his days in prayer
waiting for heaven

(rest in peace now dear Gabriel)

on great wide wings
he sees the big picture
from high above
I wander the woods
cloven-hoofed on the earth

at daybreak
the dandelions yellow
had turned to white
by noon, the seed heads flown –
is it thus, with us?

the first bird
in the pink morning light
a young magpie
drinking at the water bowl –
'one for sorrow'

small hedge sparrow
picking in the seed heads
you know nothing
of politics, wars, religion
... I wish I was you

the child on the bank
waves her hand
to the smooth-hound shark
making its sinuous way
down the river to the sea

the little jizo
stands close beside
the pale ash wand
who is to say
where magic might hide?

wasps and bees
butterflies and birds
at the water bowl
at least we are saving
some small lives

who says
they are just weeds?
they are sunshine
and seeds, to feed
the gathering birds

the water flies
when the birds bathe
and lo and behold
out of the brick weave ...
violets

all over Europe
wildfires are raging
homes burning –
man is reaping
what he has sown

the great plans
of the people in power
have shattered
leaving debris and shards
all over the quiet ground

when the world
presses in with noise
and chaos
I watch seed heads in the wind
and dream of green hills

the brick weave
crawls with big stinging ants
help is at hand
two young jackdaws
come and feast

I woke before dawn
to a blackbird singing
and in the shadows
where yesterday was dry grass –
one bright dandelion

I struggled all day
to hold on to hope
then in the night
came a nurse carrying
life in her pale hands

reading Zhuangzi
I travel back in time
two millennia
and five thousand miles
and deep inside myself

in the bamboo hut
a man with a Viking tattoo
runes and ravens
ancient words, trees
and mysteries

(Steve)

wrestling with sense
I tell myself
my daughter is gone –
inside myself, a voice says
'are you crazy?'

Olivia is dead
and I think back
to Grease
and then Hair, Godspell
Jesus Christ Superstar

the moon
almost full
and low in the sky
I sit making
impossible wishes

I love the mouse
and the pika
and the whale
and all creatures
great and small

the Sturgeon Moon
shines in my window
and I'm by the Great Lakes
watching the wild schools
of small silver fry

I look at the moon
and I hear her voice
'I am light
watch me shine'
and my heart breaks again

the one-legged
ancient music spirits
in the misty hills
drum, hopping,
singing *kui – kui*

(Kui is a figure in ancient Chinese mythology.
Classic texts use this name for the legendary
musician **Kui** who invented music and dancing;
for the one-legged mountain demon or rain-
god **Kui)**

erigeron canadensis
Canadian horseweed
appears by my window –
did her free spirit
drop the seed there?

the gardener
negotiates
a swap –
a day of tree trimming
for the old trek mountain bike

two am
we're woken by a cat fight
in the lane
and a bunch of rowdy youths –
Dales is not a peaceful Place

he says
that when his son
was in the womb
the boy grew around himself
a thick cloud of empathy

(Dave about Jake)

I wish
that I too could learn
'in whatever state
I find myself
therewith to be content'

(Philippians 1 KJB)

he picked up
the little bird laying still
on the sunny path
and carried it to shade
and in a while ... it flew

when I was small
I had a stuffed bear
that growled –
not scary, but then there are
no real bears in Norfolk

counting
nine small stones
a turning place
a sacred point
an ancient holiness

the Queen is dead
it feels as if grace
and nobility
have flown, like birds
from high places

his god
is the river
my gods
are the weeds brave
in the brick weave

(Tony Marcoff)

I am glad
Grandpa Sven is not here
to see his Uppsala –
now home to drug gangs
and shootings

oils of orange
roses, cinnamon
ambergis, musk
the annointing of the cross
over our new King

King Charles III
speaking tearfully
'my mama and papa ...
and underneath
are the everlasting arms'

Deuteronomy 33:27

three times the staff
strikes the ground ...
the Queen's children stand
in silent sad vigil
around her coffin

the native tribes with colds
gathered the horseweed
and breathed and sneezed ...
I open my window
and the same thing happens

no sound
but footsteps
as the guard changes
then a small dark boy
calls out 'goodbye my Queen'

prefab buildings
where there used to be
green fields
but still ... horses and cows
on the Acle Straight pastures

war time in Norfolk
and the land girl
said to her child
'dig here – the soldiers need
potatoes for supper'

(my mum and I)

how can I sleep
with my head full of questions:
is there a God?
was there a beginning?
will there be an end?

he buries
old sheepdog Sam
under the tree
and turns back, lonely,
to the flame

(Rob, beadmaker)

he sits in the path
of a hurricane
and he hears
Tecumseh
whispering ... Ohio

(Bob Kinsley)

the clouds above me
take the shape of our old cat
Tu Fu
and I wonder
where is Li Po?

Great Yarmouth bans
the planting of fruit trees
in case apples
are used as gang weapons ...
it's N.F.N.

(Normal for Norfolk)

the spirit
of the old crone
chuckles
waving her hands
from the dark inside

feeling tired
my mantras today :
weep more
eat less chocolate
be true to myself

the poet says
'you'll be remembered
when you are gone'
I say 'I would rather live on
and be forgotten'

my teacher brother
is teaching me
how to die
with dignity
and amazing grace

my dying brother
calls all the nurses
by their names ...
we sing Vera Lynn
'we'll meet again'

we gather clothes
for the charity shop
books for the book shop
food for the food bank
trying to make sense of loss

a postcard
with the 'plains of heaven'
arrives
on my mother's birthday –
is that where she is?

I miss walking
more these days
wanting to be
closer to the earth
nearer to the centre

in a pile of books
I found one
I had forgotten
and was lost in it
most of the night

(Poems of impermanence, mindfulness and joy)

the river
is wide and deep
between life and death
and no one knows
what's on the other side

valomeri –

we light the candles
by the crosses and stones
and hope that the spirits
will see the small lights
and know they are still loved

the hymn says
'count your blessings
one by one'
to be whole, we need
to count our sorrows too

All Hallows' Eve
a wild stormy night
and the spirit
of my weary brother
is free at last

(David, rest in peace)

it is sad
that in the shop
selling
noiseless fireworks
no one bought any

I read the book
beginning to end
and then
read it from back to front ...
and loved it both ways

lacking
are the words we write
in poems
there is no way to capture
the real heart of things

I look
at a weed, a feather
and write words
but what I see there
is beyond any language

I miss her
every morning
every evening
and tears fall –
it is as it must be

my first daughter
is positive and generous
and I wish
she could teach me
to be the same

(Kate)

my second daughter
was mindful and wise
and I wish
she could have taught me
to be the same

(Wendy)

the zen cards that fell
as my brother died
'let go'
'trusting' as he travelled
to his next great 'adventure'

watching gnats
flitting about the weeds
in the sunshine
and spiders spinning threads –
mid-November, it's mad!

she says
the humming sound
is aliens
who want to talk to me
but don't speak my language

a discovery –
I rest my hand
on the warm night light
and the constant ache
in the seed pearls ... eases

when I wake
it's her birthday ...
does she know
what a blessing
she is to us all?

(Kate)

I am weary ...
he says 'sleep
and dream of colour'
I settle into brown earth
and russet fur

the old matron said
'after you lose a child
you live in two worlds –
the full, busy one
and the dark empty one'

the small train
goes by and I wake
from a dream –
a deep blue tulip
in a row of green buds

haunted
by her suffering
I tell myself
it is over now ...
still the sorrow stays

coming indoors
this cold wet evening
I saw a star fall
and heard an owl calling –
that's all it took

why after two decades
wheelchair-bound
do I suddenly
feel different, and less
than those walking by?

a sudden memory
of a baby's first cry
as I crossed the landing
and my father saying
'come and see your new brother'

(David, Cambridge, July 1948)

217

stalled amid the throng
of people singing
and dancing
I felt disabled
for the first time, and wept

it is better
to call myself
a cripple
than to use other words
that mean 'less than normal'

nothing is free
all things come
at a cost
we have to decide –
to pay, or not

in the cold churchyard
he prayed for all the dead
we have loved so much
and a squirrel ran
among the gravestones

in old Amherst
Alan said 'squirrels don't run
fluid like a wave'
I still say – and write –
to me, they do

there is a humming
in the walls of my room
day and night
how I long
for a moment's silence

if you have one or two
people in your life
who really hear
what you need to say ...
you are blessed

dad asked mum
will you marry me?
she said ... no
next day he begged again
she said – well, OK, yes

the burrneshat *
spends her long years
living on the land
for the sake of freedom
family and her own self

* sworn virgin of Albania

how odd it seems, stroking
the King Charles spaniel
and now
on the English throne
a new King Charles

sometimes there is
a tiny seed of hope
buried deep
inside a rotten fruit
and next Spring ...

whoever has
my books after me
will wonder why
some page corners are turned ...
'what did she find there?'

those Easter Island gods
are tipping and falling
and breaking
just like so many gods
that are set in sand

below
the stilling surface
after the rain
mountain minnows
in the green reeds

I turn the corners
of book pages
as if to say
this one matters ...
but who am I to say?

it is not
the words we say
that matter
it is the truth
wordless, below

last Christmas
my brother made me
a nest box
now robins are nesting there
and I wish he could see them

the crab apples
have grown soft
in the bitter frost
the Swedish fieldfares
have come to feast

there's an Arctic blast
making its way south
dumping snow and ice
on the east coast
all the way to Florida

she is so brave
taking the long flight
to India
metal valves ticking
in her kind heart

(Linda)

New Year's eve
and how we long
for the first day
of a kinder
more hopeful year

Acknowledgments

A few of these tanka have appeared in Bright Stars, Atlas Poetica, the Bamboo Hut and Skylark journals. Thank you to the editors.

Afterword

Thank you for sharing your wonderful poems with me. I have been reading them over and over.

Some are deep wells, which do not reward mere sipping. They are so purely simple, yet so much can depend upon them.

They remind me of the motes of dust upon which the like of snowflakes and hailstones can become themselves; like the grain on sand in an oyster gathers pearl.

In all these poems, your sorrow and your love entwine and reflect much more than the sum of their parts.

Denis Garrison

(rest in peace now dear friend)

About the Author

Joy was born in Norwich towards the end of WW2. She lived in several English towns in her youth as her father was a roving vicar.

Joy moved to Amherst, Massachusetts in 1966 when she married Brian who was at Amherst College, and from there on to Toronto, Canada where she later lived as a single mum with her two daughters. They moved back to Norwich a couple of decades later, where Joy met and married Andy, 30 years ago.

Her older daughter Kate lives in Canada and very sadly Joy's younger daughter Wendy has recently lost her brave battle with multiple sclerosis. Joy's younger brother David Street died this winter in Norwich after fighting his own courageous battle with cancer. Joy herself is a paraplegic amputee after an accident in 2002.

Her strength comes from her loved ones and from nature and from poetry. Her favourite old poets are Ryôkan and Frances Cornford.

Joy is a Pisces.

<>

More Books by Joy McCall
Can Be Found On Amazon

Printed in Great Britain
by Amazon

20854214R00159